AF151120

YOUR KNOWLEDGE HAS VALUE

- We will publish your bachelor's and master's thesis, essays and papers

- Your own eBook and book - sold worldwide in all relevant shops

- Earn money with each sale

Upload your text at www.GRIN.com
and publish for free

Sahar Jaafar

The Parallels between Fitzgerald's "The Great Gatsby" and Jack Kerouac's "On the Road"

GRIN Publishing

Bibliographic information published by the German National Library:

The German National Library lists this publication in the National Bibliography; detailed bibliographic data are available on the Internet at http://dnb.dnb.de .

This book is copyright material and must not be copied, reproduced, transferred, distributed, leased, licensed or publicly performed or used in any way except as specifically permitted in writing by the publishers, as allowed under the terms and conditions under which it was purchased or as strictly permitted by applicable copyright law. Any unauthorized distribution or use of this text may be a direct infringement of the author s and publisher s rights and those responsible may be liable in law accordingly.

Imprint:

Copyright © 2015 GRIN Verlag, Open Publishing GmbH
Print and binding: Books on Demand GmbH, Norderstedt Germany
ISBN: 978-3-668-00804-5

This book at GRIN:

http://www.grin.com/en/e-book/301899/the-parallels-between-fitzgerald-s-the-great-gatsby-and-jack-kerouac-s

GRIN - Your knowledge has value

Since its foundation in 1998, GRIN has specialized in publishing academic texts by students, college teachers and other academics as e-book and printed book. The website www.grin.com is an ideal platform for presenting term papers, final papers, scientific essays, dissertations and specialist books.

Visit us on the internet:

http://www.grin.com/

http://www.facebook.com/grincom

http://www.twitter.com/grin_com

Sahar Al-keshwan

English 544

19 December 2011

The parallels between Fitzgerald's *The Great Gatsby* and Jack Kerouac's *On the Road*

The concept of the American dream was a topic of interest for many writers in the mid of the twentieth century. Jack Kerouac's *On the Road* is a novel that discusses the idea of the American Dream and how it was corrupted after the end of World War II and the Cold War. During this time, the economic life in American is flourished and people began to move from the towns to the cities searching for a better life and future and pursing after wealth and money. *On the Road* seems a perfect example of embodying the reality of practicing the American Dream after the two wars. This novel is similar to F. Scott Fitzgerald's *The Great Gatsby* in many themes that are related to the corruption of the American Dream such as the American's ambition of getting married or having a relationship with a blonde girl so he can achieve the social success. Also, there is the concept of representing women as a marginal part or a sexual object for the men. In addition, the concerns and the racial there is the racial worries that prevailed the American society and from people of color and their anxiety for becoming competitive for the whites in the cities. There is also the presence of the jazz music as a reflection of the African-American background for both Jack Kerouac and Jay Gatsby and how they show it by representing for Jazz music. Not only this but also the different ways that the writers use to depict the west. This paper will discuss the parallel and the similarity between the two novels' on the American Dream.

On The Road is a novel written by Jack Kerouac who is an American writer from French –Canadian Origin. The novel was published in 1951. It tells a story of group of writers who travel across American in the mid of twentieth century. Also, it traces the trip of two character Sal Paradise and Dean Moriarty who travel across America,first from New York to the West Coast and then to Mexico. Through their journey, they try to behave freely and practice all kind of entertainment: sex, drugs, and music without paying attention to the reaction of the society towards their behavior; therefore they are called the ˙Beat Generation˙ which is a movement fora group of writers who are taken by sex, drugs, and alcohol, but also

1

are inspired by the Eastern religion and culture. In fact, the novel also reflects a true story of the tripof Jack Kerouac and his friend Neal Cassady. The novel itself is a form of letters between Jack Kerouac and Neal Cassady. Then, Kerouac conveyed these letters to anovel which was written in three weeks.

In addition to the main plot of the novel, it also represents the main ideologies that this movement is based on the protest against the material, industrial life in America after WWII in 1950s. During the post war era, the economic situation in America began to be stronger than before. The Americans pay their attention toward a better life by trying to develop their economic situation. However, they lost communication with each other for they go toward the East: New York and California as are of the main cities of Industry. Shortly, they move from the simple and natural life in the west towards the east. During this time, the west became a place for poor people and those who are not interested in the industrial life; therefore, this situation created inequality among the states. Some people were prevented from many chances and jobs. Therefore the better life and equal opportunities which represents the meaning of the American Dream were not there. The American Dream which states that "life should be better and richer and fuller for everyone, with opportunity for each according to ability or achievement" was not achieved. Jack Kerouac as a member of the beat generation and his travel as an outlaw adventures serves as protest to this life. Beside self-invention and pleasure, there was the protest on the fall of the American Dream.

F. Scott Fitzgerald's *The Great Gatsby* is also a novel which discusses the achievement of the American Dream. Nick Carraway, the narrator of this story move from the West Egg to the East Egg for a business bond. He meets Gatsby, a wealthy man who also moves from the west to the east for pursuing after wealth. Gatsby also moves to the east to bring his love, Daisy, back again who is married to another manto bring back Daisy, the woman whom he loves, and who is now married to another man, Tom Buchanan. However, this novel is devoted for the pursuing of the American Dream. In addition, it shows the way that the Americans like Gatsby and Nick Carraway practices the ideology of it to whom you refer by it by making money and move to industrial cities like New York. That means the opportunities are also absent in the West. Since this novel also discusses the American Dream, I found alto of themes that are similar to Kerouac's *On the Road*'s themes. These themes are concerned with the idea the sexual purity and that the social success is connected of getting married of or having sex with blonde woman, The possibility of the African-American background for both Jack Kerouac and Jay Gatsby and the racial issues that they

2

both had while moving to and from the west. The view of the writers: Kerouac and Fitzgerald from the African-Americans. It includes also a similarity between Gatsby's ambition and Dean Mortiarty's one in moving to New York and pursuing after wealth there. This paper will discuss the similarity and contradiction between these themes.

The first parallel theme between the two novels is that both of Sal Paradise and Jay Gatsby want to get married to a blonde girl. They aspire to be in relation with a blonde woman, because that will lead them to achieve the social success. It is the sexual purity that shapes the American mind after the WWI and WWII. In *On the Road*, All the desired females in this novel are blondes. There is Beverly, Bob Burford's sister whose Sal Paradise always describes her as beautiful blonde woman. There is another girl whose Sal "spent a whole night with [her] on a parkbench…she was a blonde from Mennisota" (66). The description itself of the blonde girl is different from the description of girl of color. Sal says describing one of the blonde girl as she "look up with a mild wonder". In New York, there are "two colored girl" that are supposed to meet with Dean and Jack but they "didn't show up" (6). Even this sentence gives the sense of the marginal role that the woman of color has. While the blonde woman is desired from the men and she is desired even from the Beat Generation whom values rejects such racial issues. Nancy McCampbell Grace, a critic, argues that Kerouac's ideal woman, the blonde woman who is shown in many writing such as "'The White American Woman,' or 'the Good Blonde'" reflects the writer's interest in deifying her, because "pure and beautiful, a trophy wife or girlfriend signifying economic, social, and spiritual success," (41). He conveys this concept in order toshow the corrupted thoughts that some of the American has in the mid-twentieth century from pursuing after the blonde woman who represents the social success and neglect woman of color who represents the marginalized woman (Grace 41).

Unlike Kerouac, Gatsby does not make a critique on the American identity. Gatsby means to move to the east to bring back his love, Daisy who is a blonde girl in order to achieve the social success as he is married of a blonde white American girl. Gatsby who is either Jewish or black desires to be a white man. His love for Daisy represents his love for the whiteness and the white society. Gatsby is not like Kerouac melts in the risky American identity, but he means to be a white pure American. Nevertheless it is the isolation and the racial and social worries after the Cold War and World War One that creates such images in the two novels.

3

However, despite depicting the blonde as being the more desired than the girl of color, the woman in general in Kerouac's works are either marginalized or sex objects. The woman in Kerouac's works appears only as a housewife, a labor, or a sexual figure. in her article, Grace also argues this notion by mentioning Kerouac's refer for "fellaheen" as a word for " 'wailing humanity' as [Kerouac] called them in *On the Road* …the fellaheen is a subset of the primitive, a category to which the western culture has historically relegated blacks, women, and the feminine" (41). Like Gatsby, the woman is also considered an object for men and society. She appears as a game for the man and she aspires to get married to a wealthy man so that she can achieve the social progress. For example, Daisy despite her love for Gatsby, she decided to get married to Tom Buchanan for his fortune. She knows that if she get married of Gatsby, she will not gain the same fancy status in the society because Gatsby is from the west who has unknown origin. That is to say he might be black or Jewish. At the same time, Myrtle, another blonde character is killed at the end of the novel as her husband discovers that she has a relationship with Tom. For Tom, Myrtle is just a sex object too.

Additionally, there is another theme that both of the writers share but with different view and opinion. It is the racial worries of the African Americans which does not pursue the ideology of the American Dream. The American Dream means that all men are equal. However, in both of the novels, there is misinterpretation from the Americans to the American Dream. The white society has fears from the blacks. To illustrate, Nick Carraway in *The Great Gatsby,* describes the black people as "bucks" which is a word as one critic, Carlyle Van, Thompson, "that within white supremacist discourse figures the black man as a sexual menace. The sexually racist term signifies a territory between human and animal and thus eschews specificity even while marking it" (70). Nick says "As we crossed Blackwell's Island a limousine passed us, driven by a white chauffeur, in which thee sat three modish Negroes, two bucks and a girl" (69). Nick makes fun of the African Americans in the same time he is afraid of the possibility of being superior in the White society as he sees them "driven by a white chauffeur". However, this scene appears with using the same word "buck" in when he describes the boys with this word as he is trying to sell him a black tea. In *On the Road*, Kerouac gives a lot of brutal discretions for the blacks, first he describes them as a Negro which is a term that refer to discrimination. Second, he gives brutal pictures about them for example as they steal the money. In one of the scenes, Kerouac says "a couple of negro characters whispered in my ear about tea. One buck. I said Okay…he had my dollar already" (81). This image as one critic says, Grace, is depicted to show again how the

Americans perceive the blacks. He did not depict them superior in the novel. Rather he depicts them brutal. However, there is another critic who has a different point of view. Jon Panish argues that the use of the term Negro refers to Kerouac's "primitivizing and romanticizing the experiences of racial minorities… in the purpose of enhancing their own position as white outsiders" (108). The using of the word Negro seems to romanticize them to help them get their rights; especially that this novel was published in fifties in coincidence with theCivil Right Movement in 1950s. However, Grace says that Kerouac uses the "black person as a bound and/or rejected, to reflect on humanity, specifically the risky venture of exploring of 'one's own body in the guise of the sexuality, vulnerability, and anarchy of the other'" (qtd. in Grace 40).

Moreover, the protagonists in both novels share the feeling of nostalgia to Jazz music. Like Gatsby whose Jazz music represents an in heritage of his culture and part of his culture as he might be a black, Kerouac also use Jazz music. There could be a connection though between The Great Gatsby and On the Road, it is the jazz music and the nostalgia to this kind of music. Like Gatsby, Kerouac also uses jazz music to represent his inheritance and cultural background as he is non- white, a French man. It represents him as he an outcast man by the non-whites people. In his critical essay, Douglas Malcolm argues indeed that Kerouac uses Jazz music because "of its ideological association with African-American culture" (94). Kerouac uses this kind of music in his novel to reflect himself and his group as outsiders who are isolated from the rest of the society. Indeed, this shows how the society looks at them as they are from another culture or their origin is from another country. Again, just like his descriptions for the African-American as "Negros" implies his method romanticizing them as they also have the right and have a part of this society, Kerouac by his using for Jazz music also reflects his romanticizing for the African-American in the same time he is primitivizing them.

However, Kerouac's depiction for Jazz music as "madness" besides his primitivizing the African- American, also wants to convey the view of the society towards them. In *on the Raod*, Paradise depicts this image in saying that he "never saw such crazy musician" (177).In the same article, Malcolm says that Kerouac's use for the word madness reflects the ideology of the white society on Jazz music that it "derives not so much from bop itself as from white cultural assumptions about music and about black culture" (97).

5

The only difference here is that Kerouac moves from the East: New York towards the West coast because he finds that life there is simpler. He finds the American Dream in being with people and in community. Moreover, he finds the almighty America in the West land where the mountain and nature are there. The American Dream for Kerouac is not in the city but in the West's town. It is in nature where all people are together and share their life with each other. The situation is different from Gatsby. The corruption of the American Dream appears when Gatsby decided to move from the West Egg to the East Egg.

The end of the two novels has a lot of similarities. In the end, both of the writers depicts the corruption of American Dream: In the Great Gatsby by Gatsby's death and in On the Road by "the sun [when] it goes down". Moreover, as once critic, Richard William says that both of the writers ended with the same aim but with different setting. He says "both narrators reflect on their experiences of the United States. Fitzgerald and Kerouac divide their final pages into (a) the setting for meditation, (b) the places meditated on, (c) the time of day when each meditation takes places, (d) the meditation on America's history, and (e) a reflection of the American people" (209). Indeed, Fitzgerald's view of the future of the American Dream is more optimistic than Jack Kerouac. He ends his novel by saying that:

"Gatsby believed in the green light, the orgastic future that year by year recedes before us. It eluded us then, but that's no matter- to-morrow we will run faster, stretch out our arms farther....And one fine morning- So we beat on, boats against the current, borne back ceaselessly into the past" (180).

On the one hand, Fitzgerald still believes that the American Dream can be achieved one day and all men will be equal. On the other hand, the end of Jack Kerouac's novel is pessimistic and reflects his despair of achieving the American Dream. In the end, Sal sits "on the old broken-down river watching...the coming of complete night that blesses the earth, darkens all rivers, cups the peaks and folds the final shore in, and nobody, nobody knows what's going to happen to anybody bedsides the forlorn rags of growing old" (293)

Indeed there is a big difference between the views of the two writers. Kerouac does not see but the darkness and night that prevails America, while Fitzgerald depicts the optimistic picture of Gatsby when he still dreams of Daisy's coming back to him. In contrast, Sal in the darkness on the river still remember Dean Moriarty whose Sal does not know the reason for his staying in the East in New York "ragged in a motheaten overcoat he brought specially for the freezing temperatures of the East, walked off alone, and the last [Sal] saw of him he rounded the corner of Seventh Avenue, eyes on the street ahead, and bent to it again" (292). There is no reason for Dean's existence in New York where he is sad and unknown life and ambitions, while Gatsby believes that Daisy still loves him and she will return to him someday.

In the end, both of the writers: Jack Kerouac and F. Scott Fitzgerald have a deep insight ofperceivingthe American Dream and its corruption by the misinterpretation of people. The American Dream should mean all men all equal in opportunity, but people in America after World War II and World War I misuse the meaning of it and understood it as a competition among people for getting money and pursuing after wealth. Jack Kerouac and F. Scott Fitzgerald find many critical aspects that reflect the misconception of the ideology of the American Dream. They mention that the men desire the blonde woman as a way to achieve a social success. Pal in On the Road have sex with many blonde girl while the other girls of color are marginalized. In *The Great Gatsby*, Gatsby dreams to get married of Daisy, the blonde woman, so as also to achieve a social and economic success. Despite this picture of the blonde woman, both of the writers depict the woman either as a sexual object or as a marginalized woman and housewives. The writers also wants to show the anxiety that the Americans feel from people of color, specifically the African-Americans so they called them as "bucks" such as in Fitzgerald's *The Great Gatsby* or as a "Negro" such as Jack Kerouac's *On the Road* . However, unlike Fitzgerald who himself have anxiety from the African-Americans based on historical documents, Kerouac uses this term to romanticize them so they can win people's sympathy for having their rights. Besides the anxiety of the African-Americans, there is a representation for Jazz music as part of their history. It is part of Gatsby's background and it is part of Kerouac's background as he is considered a non-white even if he is French. Nevertheless, they share the same end as Gatsby is looking at the green light and Sal is sitting on the river. However, Kerouac is more pessimistic about the future of America as he depicts Sal watching the darkness prevail the west land. Conversely, Fitzgerald is looking to anew future after Gatsby's death. Indeed, Kerouac is inspired by Fitzgerald's critique for the American Dream and he was creative in applying the same notion with his travel writing. Jack Kerouac succeeded in criticizing the misinterpretation of the Americans for the American Dream.

Works Cited

"'Jazz American': Jazz And African American Culture In Jack Kerouac's On The Road." *Contemporary Literature* 40.1(1999): 85. *Academic Search Complete*.Web. 2011.

Grace, Nancy McCampbell. "A white Man In Love: A Study of Race, Gender, Class, And Ethnicity In Jack Kerouac's Maggie Cassidy, The Subterraneans, And Tristessa." *College Literature* 27.1(2000):39. *Academic Search Complete*.Web.18 Dec.2011.

Kerouac, Jack, and Scott Donaldson. *On the Road*. New York: Penguin Books, 1979. Print.

Fitzgerald, F S, and Matthew J. Bruccoli. *The Great Gatsby*. Cambridge: Cambridge University Press, 1991. Print.

Panish, Jon. "Kerouac's The Subterraneans: A Study Of 'Romantic Primitivism'." Melus 19.3 (1994):107. Academic Search Complete.Web.18 Dec.2011.

Thompson, Carlyle Van. "The Tragic Black Buck: Jay Gatsby's Passing in F. Scott Fitzgerald's *The Great Gatsby*."*The Tragic Black Buck: Racial Masquerading in the American Literary Imagination*. New York: Peter Lang, 2004. 75-103. Print.